Author:
Jacqueline Morley studied English at Oxford
University. She has taught English and History and
has a special interest in the history of everyday
life. She has written historical fiction and non-
fiction for children and is the author of the
prizewinning **An Egyptian Pyramid** in the *Inside
Story* series.

Artist:
David Antram was born in Brighton, England,
in 1958. He studied at Eastbourne College of Art
and then worked in advertising for fifteen years
before becoming a full-time artist. He has
illustrated many children's non-fiction books.

Series Creator:
David Salariya was born in Dundee, Scotland.
He has illustrated a wide range of books and has
created and designed many new series for
publishers both in the UK and overseas. In 1989,
he established The Salariya Book Company. He
lives in Brighton with his wife, illustrator Shirley
Willis, and their son Jonathan.

Editor: **Michael Ford**

Assistant Editor: **Charlene Dobson**

Published in Great Britain in 2004 by
Book House, an imprint of
The Salariya Book Company Ltd
25 Marlborough Place, Brighton BN1 1UB

Please visit the Salariya Book Company at:
www.salariya.com
www.book-house.co.uk

ISBN 1 904642 16 0

A catalogue record for this book is available
from the British Library.

Printed and bound in Belgium.
Printed on paper from sustainable forests.

Avoid being a Tudor Colonist!

The Danger Zone

Written by
Jacqueline Morley

Illustrated by
David Antram

Created and designed by
David Salariya

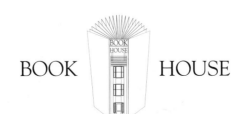

BOOK HOUSE

Contents

Introduction

It's the end of the sixteenth century and Elizabeth I is queen of England. She has defended England against Spain, the biggest power in Europe. Spain is strong and very rich with vast silver mines in America, the new land discovered by Christopher Columbus a century ago. The Spanish funded his voyages and claimed America as theirs.

But America is enormous and Spain can't control it all. The French, Dutch and English are there too, exploring the north and staying out of Spain's way. They also want America's gold and silver. This sounds good to you. You want to join the next trip to start an English colony. But if you knew what hardships and struggles lay ahead, you certainly wouldn't want to be an American colonist!

Colonist sea routes, c 1607

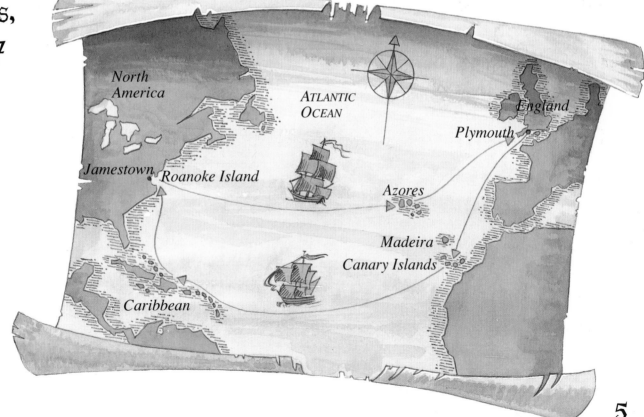

North America

ATLANTIC OCEAN

England

Plymouth

Jamestown Roanoke Island

Azores

Madeira

Canary Islands

Caribbean

5

Virginia – a bit of history

Walter Raleigh is Queen Elizabeth's favourite courtier. He tells her he has found the perfect site for the colony she hopes to set up in America. He sends out an exploratory mission and it returns with glowing reports of a warm, fertile spot on the North Atlantic shores of America, well clear of any Spanish settlement. The Queen is delighted. She dubs Raleigh a knight and declares that the new territory will be named Virginia (in her honour, for she is known as the 'Virgin Queen'). Raleigh gathers an expedition of around 500 settlers that sets sail in 1585. But their colony isn't a success. What goes wrong?

Rise, Sir Walter, and tell me of this paradise.

THE RIGHT SITE. Raleigh knows he has to find a site first. In 1583 his half-brother had set off with 260 men, but with no idea where to land. He drowned at sea.

Handy hint
To persuade people to fund a trip, suggest that they will make a fortune from capturing Spanish cargo ships along the way.

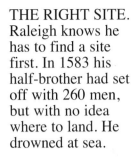

PARADISE FOUND? The men Raleigh sent to find a site describe America as a paradise with ripe grapes growing wild and peopled with friendly natives.

NATIVES. They bring two of these native people back to England to learn their language. Londoners stare at them in amazement.

SEVEN SHIPS. Raleigh raises a fleet of seven ships to take his colonists across the Atlantic. He does not go himself, but puts two tough, experienced commanders in charge.

The lost colony

Raleigh's colonists settle on an island called Roanoke. They bully the native Algonquin tribe for food and to find out where gold can be found. They take hostages and burn villages. But when a supply ship doesn't arrive, the colonists sail home. In 1587, a second expedition, led by John White, includes women. The Algonquins are hostile, so White sails home for supplies. The colonists left behind are told to leave a message if they desert the settlement. When White returns three years later, he finds the buildings torn down and the settlement abandoned. The word 'Croatoan' has been carved on a post, but nobody knows what has happened to the colonists.

RECKLESS ACTS. When friendly Algonquins steal a settler's cup, the hot-headed leaders of the first trip destroy their village and burn all their crops.

REVENGE. The Algonquins do not forgive. One of White's team is shot with 16 arrows while fishing for crabs.

Whoosh

FIRST BABY. White's daughter has a baby at Roanoke and names her Virginia. She is the first English colonist born in America.

Bawl

Provisions you'll need:

The voyage out

It's 1606 and, despite the Roanoke disaster, some optimistic London merchants form the Virginia Company to finance a trading colony in Virginia. They are sending out three ships, the largest only 22 m long, and you are one of 144 settlers crammed on board. With the heaving Atlantic threatening to swamp the boat, you're already thinking this was a bad decision. If you're lucky, you will spend two months at sea, but the trip can take up to six months if storms drive your ship off its course.

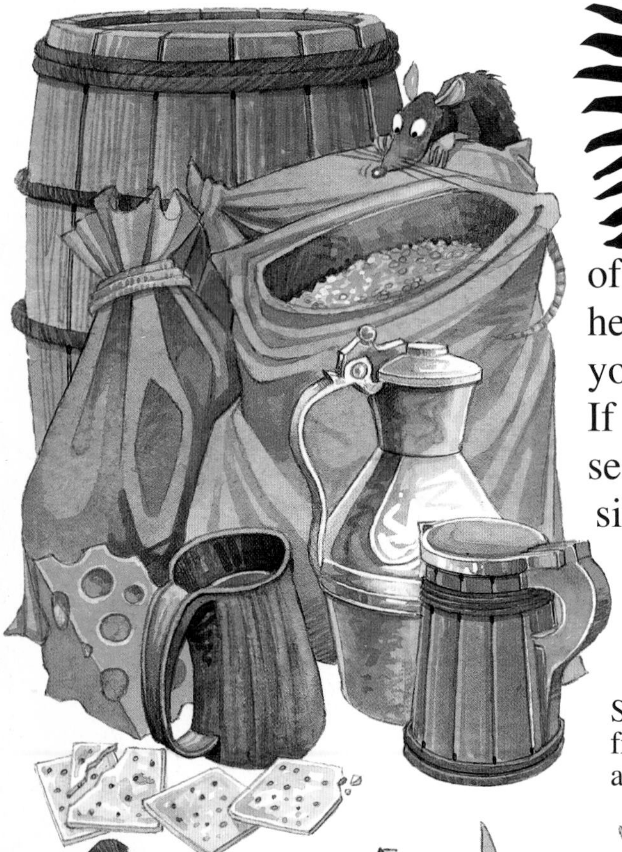

SALTED MEAT and fish, dried fruit, beans and hard biscuits are all you eat.

FRESH SUPPLIES. The ships take a southerly route via the Caribbean Islands. Here you can buy fresh fruit, vegetables and meat.

Mooooo

Cluck Cluck

Snort

10

At least you're not paying for this terrible journey. Those colonists who do pay will be given land in the new colony. You can't afford the fare, so you have undertaken to serve the Company for seven years instead. You don't get any favours – you sleep on the floor of the smelly lower deck.

Third time lucky?

April 1607 – Virginia at last! The ships explore a river to find a good place to settle. The leaders argue all the time, despite clear orders from the Company. The site must be healthy, fertile and easy to defend. It needs a clear view of ships approaching from the sea, in case the Spanish attack. Luckily, they find a place where ships can moor close to the bank. The land is low and unoccupied. It's almost like an island, so it's hard to attack from land. This makes it ideal.

That way...

No, this way, you fool!

Handy hint

If you find a place that local people don't seem to want, ask yourself why. There may be drawbacks you don't notice.

GET RICH QUICK. Some colonists won't do heavy work. They are 'gentlemen' and in England they didn't have to work. They've come to make a quick fortune from gold and won't obey orders.

Problems with the site:

SWAMP LAND. Most of the land is swamp. The rest consists of a thin layer of good soil over muddy clay.

CRAZY CLIMATE. The weather is unpredictable – hot and humid, with sudden violent winds and thunderstorms.

MOSQUITOES, breeding in the swamps, carry deadly yellow fever. No-one realises this at the time.

Settling in

The new settlement is to be called Jamestown after England's new king, James I. Tents are put up and the work begins. Soon your hands blister and bleed from felling trees. You're not used to all this hard work! The aim is to build a strong fort. In the first few days the colony was almost wiped out. Two hundred Algonquin warriors launched an ambush while everyone was working and unarmed. You would all be dead now if cannons fired from the ships had not scared them off.

UNDER ATTACK. A tent offers no protection. A man and a boy are killed and 10 colonists are wounded when the camp is attacked.

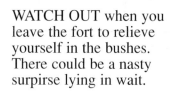

WATCH OUT when you leave the fort to relieve yourself in the bushes. There could be a nasty surpirse lying in wait.

ARMOUR IS USELESS. It's hot and very heavy to wear. The noise it makes tells the enemy exactly where you are.

Handy hint

Take advice from friendly locals. One suggestion is to cut the long grass around the fort because enemies can hide there.

I thought I was coming to a paradise!

Oops!

SPANISH INVASION. Hostile neighbours are not the only worry. Cannons are now mounted at each corner of the fort in case the Spaniards attack.

DEATH TOLL. Many colonists fall sick from yellow fever or by drinking polluted water from the river. By September half of them are dead.

LEADERS QUARREL and accuse each other of plotting rebellions within the colony. One of them is tried, found guilty and shot.

The Algonquins – friends or foes?

You soon discover people called the Algonquins who live nearby. There are many different tribes that live in villages. They build houses out of bark or matting attached to a framework of poles. They hunt, fish and farm – they grow sweetcorn (a plant that's new to you), which is their main food source. They do not know how to make metal or glass, so they are fascinated by the knives and colourful glass beads you bring to trade. Friendlier tribes are eager to exchange food for these shiny trinkets – at first.

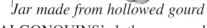
Jar made from hollowed gourd

ALGONQUINS' clothes are made of animal skins. The woman has her arm in a sling set with tiny shells. The shells are used as money.

WOMEN DO THE FARMING and weed the corn. One hides in a shelter to scare birds away.

ENGLISH WAYS of farming do not work here. Ploughs snag on tree roots and wheat won't sprout.

STARVING. Winter comes and you have no food. The Algonquins have none to spare.

A CAPTIVE shows you how to grow corn – plant just a few seeds in mounds of soil.

Exploring the territory

Exploration is part of your job. The Virginia Company wants to make lots of money. It expects the colonists to discover where gold can be mined and to find the great lake that everyone believes to be a short cut to China!

A team led by a fiery and tough-minded colonist, Captain John Smith, go out to explore. He returns with a hair-raising story. Captured and condemned to have his brains beaten out, he is saved in the nick of time by an Algonquin princess who begs her father to spare his life.

The adventures of John Smith:

1. EXPLORING a narrow river, the team's barge is halted by overhanging branches. Smith then decides to go on by canoe.

2. AMBUSHED by hostile bowmen, Smith uses his guide (a friendly Algonquin) as a shield. He manages to escape, but is captured when he falls into a bog.

3. TAKEN PRISONER. The captured Smith is paraded around villages by dancing warriors, who lead him to the court of the great chief Powhatan.

4. POWHATAN, the mighty overlord of many tribes, believes colonists are a threat to his people. After questioning Smith, he condemns him to death by clubbing.

Handy hint

Impress your captors with your 'magic'. Smith shows them his compass which 'knows' where north is.

Put down your clubs.

Gulp!

SAVED! As the executioners raise their clubs, Powhatan's young daughter Pocahontas throws herself on Smith to protect him. Taking this as an omen, Powhatan spares his life and swears that Smith is his brother from now on.

19

Supply ships – a blessing or a curse?

The Virginia Company sends out supply ships to the colony. Bad weather can delay them for months and some never arrive at all. When they do, you may wish they hadn't. Their crews don't know how hard life can be over here. The captain of the first ship stays for 14 weeks looking for gold. He keeps his crew fed all this time on supplies meant for you. The crew spend their time trading with the Algonquins and, having much more to offer than the colonists, they drive the price of local food sky-high. You are glad to see them go. Next comes a shipment of new settlers, mostly unskilled – just more useless extra mouths to feed when you're already almost starving!

TROUBLE. Some new arrivals look like troublemakers that England wants to get rid of. They come over expecting an easy life.

RATIONS. In England, the new settlers heard that everything is going well at Jamestown. The daily ration of boiled barley comes as a shock to them.

NO GOLD. No-one finds any gold. Rocks sent home for testing prove worthless. The captain has no luck panning the river for gold either.

TOOLS FOR FOOD. Many tools disappear from the fort's store. Desperate colonists steal them to buy food from the sailors.

The struggle to survive

Captain Smith is in charge now. Unlike previous leaders, he makes even the laziest gentlemen sweat hard – building, clearing, planting fields and digging a proper well. The colony also has to satisfy the Virginia Company, which is demanding goods to sell in England to cover the cost of sending you supplies. Timber is the only raw material. You turn it into clapboard to send home on the next voyage.

Setbacks:

JANUARY 1608. A terrible fire somehow breaks out in the fort. Almost all the buildings are destroyed and need to be rebuilt.

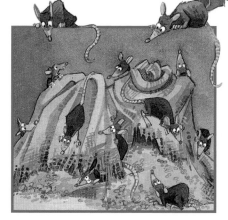

BROWN RATS that escaped from the supply ships have bred in huge numbers. They eat half the corn reserves in the store.

SPRING 1609. Food is so scarce that Smith sends a third of the colonists down the river to see if they can live on oysters from the riverbed.

Handy hint
Keep a fishing net handy – you won't catch many fish with your frying pan.

HARD TIMES. Explorations go on, but life is hard when you're huddled under tarpaulin – cold, wet and in fear of enemies all around.

STRANGE CREATURES. You never know what you'll meet in a strange land. When Captain Smith is stung by a stingray, it is so painful he thinks he is dying.

FINAL DEMAND. In a furious letter, Smith tells the Virginia Company to send him people with useful skills and that the trees are not suitable for clapboard.

23

Famine and starvation

I t's Winter 1609. A drought has made the crops fail. The Algonquins have little to eat and there's no food at Jamestown. The store is empty and raiding the Algonquins for food has made them bitter enemies. You've eaten the horses, dogs, cats and rats. You've even boiled your boots, belts and every scrap of leather for food! People stagger into the woods in search of snakes or edible roots. Most will never return. You bury bodies daily and you even suspect that some colonists will dig them up again to eat!

YOU CAN DIE of famine in the safety of the fort or risk your life outside in search of food. Algonquin warriors are waiting to pick you off.

BROKEN PROMISES. Smith has had to return to England and Powhatan is no longer friendly. He won't sell you corn and aims to drive the colonists from the land.

WARNINGS. Colonists who try to steal corn are found dead, their throats stuffed with bread. It's a warning from the Algonquins.

24

HUNGER drives some people mad. A man is convicted for killing his wife. He chopped her up, salted the pieces and ate quite a lot of her before he was found out. His sentence is to be burned alive.

Handy hint

When you've eaten your horse, don't waste its hide and hooves. Boil them up for stew.

I wish I was home!

The colony grows

Years have passed and you no longer work for the Virginia Company. You buy some land in one of the new settlements along the river, beyond Jamestown. Many new settlers buy land there to farm. But the Company doesn't really own the land it is selling. It has seized it from the Algonquins. If a tribe is hostile, its village is destroyed, so it's safer for tribes to seem friendly. But secretly they are plotting to wipe out the white men. In March 1622, they massacre colonists all along the river. It is thanks to a warning from a friendly Algonquin that Jamestown is saved from total destruction.

What was behind the Indians' hostility?

SETTLEMENTS are well protected with palisaded forts and storehouses. Fields are fenced off and each house has an enclosed yard for livestock.

ANGER GROWS as the Algonquins see more of their land being fenced off. They are told they cannot enter it without permission.

IN 1622, friendly-looking Algonquin traders are invited in for breakfast. But suddenly they seize their hosts' tools and attack.

We want our land back!

Handy hint

At the first sign of trouble from hostile tribes, run for the safety of the fort.

Gotcha!

IN RUINS. People are killed in their homes and in the fields. The colonists' houses are burned down and they are slaughtered.

Making a go of it

Congratulations! You've worked hard to build yourself a home. Now you have a thriving farm. Life is getting easier. The Algonquins seem to be beaten and the colony has found a money-spinner – exporting tobacco to Europe. Local Virginian tobacco is not much good, but a colonist called John Rolfe experiments with growing other types from Spanish America. He is so successful that now, in the 1620s, tobacco is the colony's chief crop. You aim to make your fortune from it. The future looks good, but remember that

TOBACCO SMOKING reaches Europe from America in the 16th Century. King James I thinks it's a filthy, harmful habit.

you have been lucky. In the colony's first 18 years, 7289 colonists sailed for Virginia and 6040 of those died. Had you known the hardships you would face, would you still have wanted to be an American colonist?

IN THE 1620S Jamestown is a thriving little market town. People no longer fear living outside the fort. Now it is the Algonquins who are fearful.

INDEPENDENCE. Virginia makes its own laws. King James I is against this, but in 1619 the colonists hold the first elected 'parliament' in the New World.

Glossary

Algonquins The Algonquin-speaking Indian tribe that lived along the eastern side of North America, as far as the Great Lakes.

Ambush A surprise attack from a hidden position.

Armada The powerful Spanish fleet that invaded England in 1588, but was defeated by the English and the Dutch.

Cannon A large gun that is fixed on a platform for firing because of its size.

Clapboard Thin wooden boards for building, made by splitting timber vertically.

Colony A group of people who settle in a country far from their homeland.

Condemned When someone is found guilty of a crime and is given punishment for it.

Courtier A servant of a royal court.

Dubbing When a king or queen makes one of their subjects a knight, giving him the title 'Sir'.

Drought A lack of water causing crops to fail.

Felling Cutting and knocking down something, such as a tree.

Fort A settlement enclosed by protective walls, with a guarded gate, which can easily be defended.

Gentleman A man born into a family, which, unlike ordinary families, had the right to carry arms.

Gourd The large, hard-skinned fruit of a trailing plant – similar to a pumpkin.

Massacre When a large number of people are killed.

Money-spinner An idea, person or thing that is a source of wealth.

Native Someone who is living in the place they were born.

Omen A sign of future happiness or disaster.

Palisade A strong, tall fence made of close-set wooden stakes.

Panning Searching for gold by rinsing soil in a pan to separate any particles of gold it may contain.

Publicity Getting people interested in someone or something.

Stingray A flat fish with a tail that injects a poison, which affects the heart and nervous system.

Tarpaulin A sheet of canvas coated with tar to make it waterproof.

Trinket A small or worthless ornament or piece of jewellery.

Yellow fever A disease that causes liver damage and turns the skin yellow.

Index